CONFLUENCE

Contents

Ohio

Monongahela

Downed Birds

I peeled open an orange.
Inside was a rotten orange,
and the rotten orange split open.
Inside: another rotten orange.
An orange, an orange, orange,
oranges—and another,
until dead oranges
spilled over my counter.

Spilling, as in the distance, the distance
spills, like wild blackbirds
pouring themselves over a horizon,
a horizon at the edge of a lake.
Like a lake pressing concrete walls
of a dam, the lake overflowing,
spilling, over the lake, spilling—the lake,
spilling the way sunset bleeds daylight
into the horizon meeting the lake.

Like a blackbird snatching up
a blackbird, a spilling blackbird
with eyes, spilling, spilling;
a blackbird with a lake
on the tip of her tongue—
like a blackbird snatching up
a rotten orange in her beak,
in the distance, a gunshot.

November

All above the gravel road,
telephone wires hover.
It is late November.
The shade is beginning to set in,
grazing the tops of the edges
of the tree branches.
Soon it will be purple, dark.

A woman's voice echoes.
She has called the police.
She is crying that John has gone missing.
This sort of thing happens.
Neither she nor the police yet know
that John has put a bullet in his head.

I speed up.
I am late to pick up the children,
and I promised I would not be late.

Hoarded Birds

And by the way, all of
this was before a tamed canary
grew very wild inside of my throat,
and I travelled as far south as Guadalajara
to find a doctor who would remove it, whole.
She shook her head, no, no,
this is a thing you must do yourself.

One morning in a dining room, maybe,
with the daybreak haloing fresh lavender
someone has arranged on the tablecloth.

There are no miracles anywhere,
unless the bird takes flight and carries us
north once more.

Bodega Mangos

I lost me on the exam table.
Me, I cracked into two bits:
today-woman and someday-woman
and one of me took off for a city
like a deer about to get run down.
I pulled on a hockey helmet
and bolted. Young girl, orange.

I found me splitting open bodega mangos,

my calloused hands sticky, shaking.
Maybe I was looking for something.
Maybe for someone I once was.
It was hot. It was evening, and I saw me
in the sidewalk. A fluorescent mosquito hiss
hovered overhead.

It was 7:49 in the evening.
I held out my hands.

Garbage Night

It is Thursday night.
It is garbage night.
The trash is my old clothes
and my old clothes are slipping through my hands.
My hands are a box full of flies.
The flies are taking off with my hair –
look! I am bald. I am my mother's truck engine.
I am the space the deer left sleeping in the ferns.
I am 7:52 in the evening.
See, the sun has already set
and the dog is crying to go out. Am I her, too?
Her nose raised, twitching, into the evening air?
My parents are getting old.
I don't like to say that out loud, but it's true.
The dog is old, too.
I am rubbing the dog's legs.
I am a car full of empty coffee cups –
see, I can't bring myself to dump them.
They remind me of yesterday.
I am all the days that the sky
has broken clear and cold,
spilling oranges across the dawn-line.
I am the Ohio line.
I am West Side Road after all the tourists
have left for the day I am
laying myself down on the asphalt
to watch the stars come out
in real soaring spires above my head
until the dog begins her howling.
I am waking all the days.
I am the ferns, and I keep space for you
for the coffee cups. I am
peeling my long body
off asphalt, and gone round back
to feed the chickens.

Thoughts on a Shallow Balcony

My mother sent me to Zelienople
to visit a sick aunt. Does it matter with what?

Sick is sick.

But Zelienople is hours from Irwin so
I veered off the Veteran's Street Bridge
into the Strip District. And there, as always,
St. Stanislaus Kostka stood stoic, a brick-lined
cathedral guarding the rows of restaurants,
gazing down at me with that great rose window,
an accusatory eye. Some priest once told me
the circle represents God, but I don't believe
in symbols anymore.

And if it's God looking down on me,
I hope He knows I just wanted to eat lunch
where the halushki tastes like fried onions and like
my grandmother's apartment, the second-to-last place
she lived. Sometimes, I would sit barefoot on her shallow,
carpeted balcony, wedged between all her neighbors,
and hear the scent of Polish cooking coming from open windows;
an old man smoking kielbasa in a bathroom,
while his wife stirred great pots of borsch on the stove.

Crossing the Hot Metal Street Bridge

It was late January and I was crossing Forbes at Fifth.
There was an old woman sitting in a folding chair there.
She was shouting that the miracle would take place
in a studio apartment in Saugerties. It was too cold
for anyone to be making prophecy that day – or any day
in January, really – but there she was, a small wonder.
I could hear her on the Hot Metal Street Bridge,
with all its spires, messy, knotted, soaring upward
into grey-lit skyline and all at once, I forgot where I was.

The old woman was my grandmother – or me.
If I lingered on the bridge too long. Everything was
a very wide dream, the lights from the windows of the sky-
scrapers expanding outward, pushing each other into stars.
This was real. As the city grew wide I crouched beneath
the towering posts to touch the rusted steel. Big Ben was dying.

On the South Side, Mike taped Friday's Trib over cracked
panes of glass at his bar but still, the old woman's voice,
seeping under the windowsill. My mother was frying
pierogies. She stepped away from the cast iron skillet
to gaze out the window where snowpack cleaved to tracks
and my father carried an old lab in his arms;
the wind, sharp on her nose that raised,
twitching, into evening air.

Unfenced

Lovely the morning-light that is me,
my feet bare hardwood I am
unfenced, full of sphagnum moss.
I am stamped lipstick and peat I am
the toll-booth change maker awake
in the howling in the dog's throat.
Time for walk, for the dog—look! A
leaf-stack on the corner of Mill Pond
and Orchard. Flat frog crushed
in the street, me, me! A girl-child, clean
dishes racked, laundry, folded, and me
unseeing any of it. A chapped finger
down the throat! How wonderful this
morning-light, singing down the bone.

Turnpike Toll-Taker

Why the man in a green shirt? See—
half asphalt, half me, toll taker
hovering over damp roads where
is the interchange, the city? I am old.
A gull over an ocean. The reckoning
brought on—my children.
Headlights live inside the third eye
of the final deer. I am nights full of
questions, motorcyclists, the last
car westbound—drivers, red-ringed eyes,
eyes, me! Awake! 1:37 in the morning I
am the fourth side of a triangle, alone.

Awake, Change-Maker

Look at me! I shouted, and I did I
saw a lonely dog who did not love
me, me! Mushrooms grown wild
in the hills, sprawling, sprawling
a mat across mats of sphagnum moss
I used to love but now I am too old
like a dog.

Awake, change maker! Quick dime-
flash slinging down the bone-slipped
palm of an old man who is that my
father? When did all of this happen?
When did we become the sheen,
the hissing lights?

My gosh sir yes here is your change—
be free in the night. I'm unsure
the turnpike, the long drive
home—if any of it will matter
come the dawn.

ALLEGHENY

Zelienople

I peeled open an orange.
It was all very much the same.
Free things never wonder when was
the rain, a wildness,
in a studio apartment in Saugerties
while I searched for my brother. It was hot.
One morning in a dining room, maybe,
pots of borsch on the stove.
A blackbird with a lake
like they all have, eventually.
It is not there for us. Nothing is here for us,
alive in the woods. She was
sitting in a folding chair there. She was
finally opening in August,
me holding a knife in my hands.
My mother sent me to Zelienople.

Old Man Dreaming

I watch a man grow old,
and it is my father.

Old man on two legs, old man dreaming.
Look, old man, where is the warm weather
you promised me when I was very young?
Everything I see is snowdrifts and plows
and the Monongahela is still frozen over,
the coal barges stuck fast in the ice.
I watch everything around me
hold its breath, very still in the winter
as the buildings hover over bridges
whose spires twang in the cold.

Macy's Closeout Sale

I am curious what newcomers think of my city,
but it is not really my city anymore. Not since I left
behind the haze of Big Ben jerseys on Forbes.
But I must have something. maybe the only thing
I have is the last flash of sunset over Macy's
in the Westmoreland Mall in the evening,
and my father is sitting beside me,
in a parking lot in summer. The lot is empty.
It is 9:30 at night, and wet. Look, this is
what the city allowed me to keep:
damp asphalt, a half-abandoned mall,
and my father, silent, waiting for me
to buckle my seat belt.

Things Like This

My father loves gas stations.
He's never told me this, but I know.
We know things like this about our fathers.
They sit us down, silent, it's evening,
early January they drive us down
to Sheetz in the ragtop Jeep *bundle up*
and we do in too-big borrowed gloves.
They push the Jeep to 40 plastic
windows rattle, too loud to hear
lingering Christmas carols
from WISH 99.7 but anyway who wants
to listen to Silent Night in January?

So we don't mind. We don't mind
rumbling along to fill the tires –
that air pump view hovers over
the turnpike onramp, Kohl's,
Kerber's Ice Cream, the potholes
on Route 30 unfilled, truckers blaring,
unhearing like our fathers who are
really deaf at this point from years
on that submarine when they were young—
when were they young? When was I young?
I don't think any of us know what we want
to be anymore, but there's joy in the open space.
And anyway, it is always dark anymore.
It's a January thing. Always our fathers
are sitting driver's side, silent, waiting for us
to buckle our seat belts.

Breezewood

How many cigarettes make me?
How many index taps, sparks
to cracked concrete?

Where you headed? A man's question—
it crystalizes in the mid-November air.
Pennsylvania winters are no place for
gas station conversation. But here we are.

A home-bound cold snap settles
over the interchange, hissing. Taco Bell—
the barely-lit sign mimics sunset.
Taco Hell—my father's voice.
I hardly remember. Like the Sunoco
sign, flickering, that has forgotten its O's—
Sunc.

Can you drown in a landlocked state?

Hey, where you headed?
        Home.
Where's home?
        Pittsburgh.
Nobody lives in Pittsburgh.

Sort of true. I was baptized
in the choppy Youghiogheny.
I breathe ice water. My mother,
waiting for me, fades into sleep.
A clear Midwestern sky freezes
deep—the voice of my father. How?

My Mother's Handwriting

The dragonfly lands in the space
between my fingers and the pause of the river.
Lonely paddle on the Androscoggin I breathe
early evening and flush of alpineglow—North,
the whisper to follow, a voice an echoing reverberation,
some call of some psalmist. The pines cast
themselves over still waters and a loon calls soft
and low and sad. She is like the sudden handwriting
of my mother, like the bent page of my brother's journal.
In the lingering echoes across the water I can hear
the tail end of North stretching one hundred miles
skimming the unbroken surface of the water
like the hawk gliding before a dive.

A gentle shake of my palm and the dragonfly
turns south and I paddle on beneath the pines
that sweep softly their arms, a call for me.
Behind there is a fox on a small island in
the middle of the river waiting patiently
for the first glimpse of the waning moon.

Door Without a Car

Now is my mother's voice
tangled in telephone wires
above golden fields all thick
with late summer wheat.
Just lingering in dusk-light
waiting, maybe, for me.

For me and my heavy weight
I am dragging behind — one foot,
then another, then wrenching
the thing forward.
One foot.
Down the wheatfield-flanked road,

dragging it, as if I were handcuffed
to a car door without
a window, just bits of glass at the edges
where someone might have broken it,
split open their cloth-wrapped knuckles.

All around me, the sky is dripping
cobalt and the last crow flies,
makes hay for his soft mattress and

there I am:

In the gaping silence,
listening for the voice of my mother
that once, through streets of
the old city, called me home from play.
But there is no voice. There is only
the cool flash of light through
bits of cracked window, as though
a late dusk could mend the glass.
There is only the dull scrape
of metal through a gravel road.

Ars Poetica

Too wonderful for my mind
the memory of the voice of my mother.

I am only an old city
with walls, with holes in my walls
ancient doors that creak and moan
when a traveler arrives at the gates
as though she approaches
soft the doors of the home of her father.

I am only pale streets
with tufts of grass at the feet of the bride
who has fled into the sands of the desert.
There is no bride,
only the cool flash of light through cracked windows
as though a late dusk could mend the glass.

I am only a rooftop,
an old rooftop, that remembers once
the footsteps, light dancing of my father
who offered the songs of a holy man
to the birds, all the birds who met
beneath my eaves to gather twigs.

I am only a doorway
where plants, plants not meant for doorways
snake green through cracks whose mouths
call a child home from play.
I am only a doorway.
I cannot remember the voice of my mother.
All of a sudden, I have grown very old.

Open, Like Me

My mother has left me
on the patio at Ianni's Pizza.
She has gone inside to pay the bill.
All of a sudden, I am very much alone.
It is evening. I am in love with the sunset
light chasing itself down Freeport Street
in Delmont through street-parked cars,
off canvas overhangs and yard signs.
The street asphalt is chipped and alive.
Look, a sign across from Ianni's hisses red
and awake in the evening, *Antiques — Open,*
something old and open and alive.
Everything is overgrown. Weeds tumble
into the sidewalk where I search for my mother
from the shaded patio. I am gentle with myself.
Something is freed. Yes. I am very much
alone in the evening.

The River is Wild

The river is called the Monongahela.
An old woman sits on the bank,
in a folding chair, fishing from her folding chair
and whispering things to the lures in her tack box.
Yes. To the jigs and spinners, stories of her old dog,
a water dog who drowned from water in the lungs.

And to the jitterbugs, jerking through rough-spun
surface of the river—a poor choice for choppy water—
she speaks; she once saw a coronation her television.
Or maybe it was her neighbor's television, through
her neighbor's window, as she perched, silent, still,
a young girl on her neighbor's unhearing porch.

The bobbins hear her. Maybe they even eavesdrop.
All around, the bush crickets chirp a song,
a late summer song.

As for me, I am no well-lived old woman,
casting my line into the wide Monongahela.
I am only one generation removed from then,
plus my hands are a box full of flies.

Instructions My Grandmother Left

In some unexpected
country, I remember a great
oak in the desert.
Dream me this, granddaughter:
your palms at the base of the tree,
the tree growing at first
conscious thought of skyline.
When they stare at your hands,
what will they see? For me, my hands
wrinkle. I grew old.

Tell me, what will you plant there?
Or bury? Don't let it be me.
Give my body to the Ohio.

Do you remember an evergreen
bound up in light? Did we do that,
with our hands?
Free the roots of the oak. For me,
do this. For me.

Why have they dressed me in this
paper gown? Why do you visit
so late?
Find yourself canned pears in my
cupboard. Feed yourself.

I lived. Maybe, when I have climbed
deep and far away, you will drag
fingers across unbroken sand.
Write my name.

The Civic Arena is Permanently Closed

Here is scorched hillscape, steel-ribbed bridges
poking through the sickly, pallid sheen of skin
that gasps and shudders, falls like my grandfather's chest
when the last creak of the fifth stair
becomes too much for his lungs.
He was a coal miner, then he was a dying man.
His name was Stanislaus and
he still remembered the mother tongue,
and he still remembered when Jaromir Jagr
played twenty seasons before I could crawl.
On the cold morning when his heart gave out,
there was a sound like a canary outside my window
and I, who would see Jaromir Jagr play thirty seasons,
watched quietly the turn of the orange sky,
ran my fingers over the spine of the horizon.
The turn of the last creak of the fifth stair
is so much a gasp, so little a dance.

Route 30

A woman on the folding step
her trailer parked on the blacktop
just behind a gas station just off
Pennsylvania Turnpike where
there are no more exits
until Ohio. Her robe open
at the front. It is hot. Skin sticky
even in early morning. She lights—
like we all do— a cigarette, waits
for the day to take up its living,
listening for the sound of truckers
blaring west, bound for Ohio, Indiana
and after that, well, she doesn't care
what comes after that.

Laundromat in Irwin

In the Laundromat on a Tuesday morning,
I find myself too young, or too old,
wondering how I wound up here,
at a Laundromat on a Tuesday morning,
with a few other people who also ended up here.

The royal wedding is playing on loop
on the only television above a row of thirty pound
washers. I am trying to get my partner to text me back.
There is no air conditioning, and it is heavy. The air.

I did not graduate from anything, or get married,
or find a job today. No one is listening to me,
my mouth open in the corner and I want to scream
across the row of blue plastic chairs. I am waiting
for my sheets to dry. The sheets are old, yellow
at the corners. The air is too heavy. Prince Harry
is kissing Meghan Markle, but the television is muted,
and I cannot hear the crowd, screaming.

Giuseppe

I was fifteen when the Latrobe Public High School Debate Team
named me jailbait. I watched the sun set that night. I watched
last light of a mocking midwinter sun stream through branches
in the parking lot, endless, and all the fumes pouring from
the bus exhaust pipes caught flickers of light. Then it was gone—
the sun. Giuseppe, my father's barber, had once told me Midwestern
sunsets are stark, sad things. *There's nothing like Pennsylvania
after the sun goes down.* And there isn't. Other places have miracles
in the night.

Blacktop

It is late August.
A half-remembered gas station
glows damp against evening air,
empty, and very quiet.
No one gets off the highway these days.

Tonight is the night
that some girl-child
feigns sleep in a trailer
parked in the third row
behind the gas station
just off the highway
where night truckers roar by,
unhearing.

Barefoot

I have never really been found.
Look, I am standing in the parking lot
of Earl's Dairy Whip, and the yellow sign
hums, a sickly glow onto my skin.
I am haloed in the evening.
All signs are pointing to me.
No one is looking.

My high school boyfriend is asking
if I want to share his bacon cheese tots
or if I want my own. My mouth is open.
It is evening, and the pickup truck's bed
is open, too, and my skin is hot to touch,
and the air is heavy with gasoline.

It is evening. Tell me: am I holy,
or just alone?

Оню

A Woman

A woman, her shoulders
covered by white sheets, near me,
near the ocean. In the sheets,
I find sand in her hair,
salt-crusted,
all crepuscular wonders,
like the final green flash of sunset.

The sheets are white.
A breeze opens, lifts words
from her journal and drops them
on her pillow.
Cracked window—she sleeps.

This is the best place for her—
tangled in sheets beneath
a midsummer sunset,
young, with full magnolias
alive in her window.

Everything I see is gold.

This is How She Loved Me:

all at once.

Once I took a train running
the Monongahela and I saw
the lights of the city flashing
through gaps of dark and cold
things that were once trees
and when I tossed my bags
from the car at the station
I saw a single house with
a single lit lamp.

How many lamps make a house?
How many houses make a home?
How many homes make a woman?

Once she gave me a bouquet
of summer lupine and
baby's breath. I wove
a crown and tucked it
inside a shoebox under
my bed. *Saving it for a*
rainy day I said and I
saw a sad smile and then
the next day   she was gone.

Strays

It is all very much the same.
You love a girl.
You are washing clothes
in a 24 hour laundromat
that doubles as a sandwich joint.
It is late, or early. It is the wrong hour.
It is 2am and there is a stray cattle dog pacing,
stalking bent moonlight between dryers.
There is howling in the parking lot.
You lose yourself in a handful of quarters,
in the fluorescent sheen of linoleum.
So it goes. Tell me,
where do we go from here?
The girl moves west, like they all do eventually.
She bends beneath the ocotillo plant.
In the sand she writes something wild
to watch it blow away in the wind.

Wild Girl

There are places I have never been
and somehow know I will never end up.
There is a room in New Mexico
with white stucco walls and a window
casting light onto the dusted bricks,
and on the bricks there is a single chair.
A mountain rises outside the window,
a deep red mountain against the blue-hued
sunset in the desert, in New Mexico, casting
evening shadows onto the house.

Who will find me at the edge?

Look: a girl, all split-boned, alone and
burrowing beneath the ocotillo plant,
trapped.

The Rain

There was very much a woman.
If that night some rain, a wildness,
had calmed, would she be strange
alive in the woods?

She, last wolf in the tundra, found
awake in the dusk beneath a twisted
tree and I could not ask her
to face me.

I only went out.
A vast open space running
beneath a bright sun.

Extra Omnes

Today I heard you moved
to cornfields near me, or near
where I once lived before
I left to find a miracle.

I remember you — smell of your
mother's sheets, inexplicable ever-there
of the sea, sharp scent of small salty
things. You wore overalls. Many things
in your pockets, living things like
a starfish nestled in your
collarbone. I found it, and now

I can see the end as it begins —
white smoke billowing over the Square
while the basilica holds its breath.
I would rather watch black smoke
over Roman rooftops for all my life
before returning home to find you

still in overalls, trussing chickens,
always, even when you are very old.
Your grandchildren, great-grandchildren,
and another woman with you,
tangled in white sheets, hands happy
to milk cows in the morning.
Her happiness, like I could never find
in cornfields.

When I am very old,
your voice — an echo like vespers
in the dusk. I will still be sitting
in my folding chair in Saint Peter's
Square, looking for angels in cracks
of bas-reliefs. "Out, all of you,

everyone out! I am waiting for
the sad sight of a miracle." That
is what I will shout.

Christmas Eve

Tonight the divine touches earth and I
scrub carpets at the Ramada,
whose threads taste like strip malls
where they sell prom dresses.

Empty upper parking garage
but café filled with sushi plastic water
bottles and lipstick stains while
Sterling Optical tops US Cellular
on the highway.

Caught in the headlights, a wire
deer. A baby leans too far
over the porch railing slips
through the slats—
the plummet to the pavement
is iced over, dark.

Too Much or Nothing at All

It is spring. I left the pumpkins
rotting outside all winter, and now
only their caved-in shells are left.
Gloveless, I toss them over a hill.
There is a gap in my screen door—
at night, the mosquitos find me alone.
What a great woman I am, nameless.
Maybe I was magnificent – once,
but maybe only once.
Now, pumpkins rot on my porch.

Anyway, who would really want
to be great? Great women are unhappy.
They don't kill spiders in their own showers
with their one Dollar Store bottles of shampoo,
or have sex in basement game rooms,
or eat Skippy straight from the jar with
a plastic spoon, late at night, braless.
Yes. I have what it takes to be average.
These are the things I tell myself at night,
alone, and quiet.

My Brother's Daughters

I am reading on a bench in Kennywood
while my brother's daughters ride
the Jackrabbit for the third time.

Children hurtle past my bench,
coated with powdered sugar and
face paint, reminding me to listen
to the cool warning of an August night.

And the Jackrabbit, it's not even
the best roller coaster in the park,
but they are enamored with the
everlasting surprise of the second bump,
the click-clack of the gears
sending them higher.

They will plead to stay late –
I've let slip that they can see the city
from the Thunderbolt's back after dark.
Yes, of course. I am still reading
The Yoga Sutras of Patanjali,
and the whole park will become
something like a deep inner peace
after the lights turn on, the lights
chasing each other along spires
of the Pitfall.

November Revisited

It is November and I don't like it.
Every tipped over garbage can—there's
light windows in my neighbor's basement
look! There's me and Zach Ligus in his
parent's basement watching Popeye
while my parents bury my first dog
on Zach's parents' land because they have
the sort of land where you can bury dogs
but you have to do it before the ground
freezes for the winter. I was in third grade.
Don't cry I thought you'll upset the dog but
the dog was already scared I saw it. I have
my own dog now and I'm not sure
she loves me but I know she loves not
being alone so maybe that's enough.
That's enough now.
A single tire on the curb.
A squirrel with its eyes.

Come Out, All You Moths

Thursday night is garbage night
my trash is old clothes my old
clothes are spilling through
my hands my hands are a box full of flies.
The flies are taking off with my hair—
look! I am bald. I am my mother's
truck engine I am the space the deer
left sleeping in the ferns.
I am 7:52 in the evening.
Babushka, come find me.
Babushka, the dog is old
and John is not.

And also, I left pumpkins
rotting outside and only
their caved-in shells are left
and the gap in my screen door –
at night, I soak my sheets.
At night, John puts a bullet
in his head! I am the dog's
shaking legs.

Come out, all you moths.
I am all the days that the sky
has broken clear, cold in the west.
I am spilling oranges across
the dawn-line, spilling, spilling,
wild blackbirds pouring themselves
over a horizon.
I am the Ohio line.
I am West Side Road after all
tourists have left for the day I am
laying my body down on the asphalt.
See, I am pumpkins and the dog
has taken up her howling.

Babushka, what does it mean
to grow old?

It is late November.
The shade is grazing the tops
of the pines and soon
it will be purple, dark.
I am peeling myself out of bed.
I am driving the car I am
driving the car I am the car.
I am late to pick up the children.
Somewhere, John is putting
a bullet in his head.
This sort of thing happens.

To grow old means really nothing
because I am growing old and the dog
is growing old and my parents
are growing old and John is not—
why? Because he didn't want to.
And maybe that's the trick. After all
who really wants to carry the dog
out into the yard on a January night
because she can't walk anymore?
Because that's the sort of thing
you have to do when you get old
and someday you'll be the dog, too.

Anyway, I speed up.
I am late to pick up the children,
and I promised I would not be late.

After the Wake

You were once a wild boy, beneath pines
but free spirits never wonder
when was the wooden bowl
on the kitchen table filled with turnips.
They are fresh but not clean, yet.

I am making footprints alongside
a very wide ocean that I cannot see.
It is not there for us. Nothing is here for us,
not even the snowpack over a patch
of backyard grass where, all at once,
you picked up the gun.

Today the ocean smells of lichen
and sphagnum moss, and it will
have us all someday with an accusatory finger
but today I am some woman
who leaves the root vegetables unwashed.

A wave filled with crepuscular wonders
has crashed on the edge of shoreline
and calls out my name—empty, empty.
I am some woman who wastes her old age.

The Misremembering

It really doesn't matter,
this wide forgetting.
All at once, my grandmother dies.
My uncle—my uncle?—
takes down the tire swing
limbed off some oak in her yard while

the old Italian man over the hill,
he won't take down his Christmas lights.
Do they cast haze on the snowpack?
It is some January. Four weeks ago,
a boy named John put a bullet in his head?

The next misremembering will bring
a remarkable return to silence.
I am old now, a dog having corralled
sheep in pressed-down fields, and I miss
the long drive to Washburn Road.

Split-Boned

My dog has a deformed rib, the vet says,
it doesn't hurt her. Maybe she bumped
into a coffee table when she was two weeks,
or played too rough with a brother.
She'll be fine. The vet continues her exam,
pulling back gums, good teeth, good dog.

Sometimes I can see the dog's back
arched, when she sleeps, and I know
it's that rib. And I really can't believe
she doesn't feel something.
Who knows? She's a good dog.

But isn't that how the whole world
opens itself before us?
It's all about a concave rib,
the day someone took us aside,
quiet, and told us to lay off the sugar.
Was it third grade for us all?
It doesn't hurt anymore, says
the whole world. We're all on diets,
avoiding the sharp edges of coffee tables.

I Told Colleen

I can't watch *Pulp Fiction* anymore. Last time I watched
Pulp Fiction it was deep August and I was real drunk
with John and Hannah, in ordinary joy. Ordinary joy is
August 23rd when the first cold snaps in evening and fall is
opening itself, clean and cool with the archer descending
behind loose-leaf oaks, oh night, the damp glowing gas
station across the street! But it wasn't all the nights. It was
a few months, tops, then John put the bullet in his head.

I can't talk more even when Colleen sits quiet, waiting for
me to speak in evening, March-drawn dusk as blue-light
slim drifts away. Life is brushing me clean, gently, as if
blowing dust off an old desk. An old desk? Come back to
me, says Colleen, but I am already cracking open her third
floor window, seeping myself under the sill,
a god, gone.

When the Wall Fell

I looked up when I heard the gates
come crashing down behind Peter,
and I watched him hurl the keys
to the kingdom toward the earth.
They landed at my feet,
shuddering metal.
And all around the gnarled wreckage
of the collapsed gate,
those who finally crossed
the open threshold sang and shouted,
and the weatherman heard something
like a storm building in the damp air.
Down below, where I sat cross-legged,
staring at the whole thing,
a woman I once loved lay down
beside me, and I, without looking,
asked if she could hear the songs.
Yes, she said, these are the years of thunder.

Kennywood Revisited

Thigh-sticking nights like these
I am bench-bound beneath that
bright-lit Ferris wheel while my
brother's daughters relive
my childhood. That's what I believe.

What did the wheel speak?
Only things by long-light glow sticks,
blue-green memory of Steve Daniels,
who I really think would have
kissed me on the phantom's revenge
senior year if everyone didn't think
I was a lesbian.

These nights aren't for me.
My arms stick, too heavy,
too slick for tank tops, but listen!
Children shrieking inside fun-houses,
a pirate-ship lurch and night
sends them higher, pitfall-lit against
the Pittsburgh skyline. It is a silhouette
that rises against the horizon, quiet,
watchful over the city and all her
accidental lesbians.

To Lead a Pig Skyward

I read a pig can't look up.
That you've got to gently
tilt their heads back
if they're going to take in
the night skies. I never
led a pig skyward late
at night in Pennsylvania.
Earthbound is probably
better. We all start
getting ideas when we
look up, and the pigs,
they always seemed so
pleased where they were,
rooting in soft earth.
No need to look up for God
when the holy was there,
beneath their trotters, cool
below the autumn archer
that was rising, lightly,
on the eastern horizon.

ACKNOWLEDGMENTS

My thanks to the following journals, in which some of these poems previously appeared:

Birch Gang Review	"Christmas Eve"
Hobart	"Giuseppe" "November Revisited"
Literary Accents	"Old Man Dreaming"
The Missouri Review	"Strays" "To Lead a Pig Skyward" "Too Much or Nothing at All"
On the Seawall	"Garbage Night"
Rust + Moth	"Downed Birds"
Street Light Press	"Hoarded Birds" "Turnpike Toll-Taker"

About the Author

Samantha DeFlitch earned her MFA from the University of New Hampshire, where she is the Associate Director of the Connors Writing Center. Her work has appeared in *The Missouri Review*, *Appalachian Review*, *On the Seawall*, and *Rust+Moth*, among others, and she is the 2018 recipient of the Dick Shea Memorial Award for Poetry, as judged by Shelley Girdner. *Confluence* is her first book. Originally from a small town outside of Pittsburgh, Pennsylvania, she currently lives in Portsmouth, New Hampshire, and is working on her second collection with the help of her corgi, Moose.